Is It a Wolf or a Coyote?

by Jeffery L. Williams

HAMERAY
PUBLISHING GROUP

Published in the United States of America
by the Hameray Publishing Group, Inc.

Copyright © 2016 Hameray Publishing Group, Inc.

Publisher: Raymond Yuen
Editor: Tara Rodriquez
Cover Designer: Anita Adams
Book Designer: Stephani Rosenstein

Photo Credits: Page i – Maxim Kulko (wolf), Matt Knoth (coyote); Page 2 – Michal Ninger; Page 3 – Volt Collection; Page 4 – Schaef71 (wolf), Brenda Carson (coyote); Page 5 – Holly Kuchera (wolf), Jeffrey B. Banke (coyote); Page 6 – Maxim Kulko; Page 7 – Matt Knoth; Page 8 – Vibe Images; Page 9 – Angel DiBilio; Page 10 – Denis Pepin; Page 11 – Derek R. Audette; Page 12 – Janusz Pienkowski; Page 13 – Eduard Kyslynskyy; Page 14 – Debbie Steinhausser; Page 15 – C_Gara; Page 16 – Tom Reichner (coyote), Daniel Korzeniewski (wolves)

All rights reserved. No part of this publication may be reproduced or transmitted in any form or by any means without permission in writing from the publisher. Reproduction of any part of this book, through photocopy, recording, or any electronic or mechanical retrieval system without the written permission of the publisher, is an infringement of the copyright law.

ISBN 978-1-62817-566-0

Printed in Singapore

1 2 3 4 5 6 7 IPS 22 21 20 19 18 17 16

Table of Contents

Size 6

Heads 8

Feet... 10

Food 12

Hunting 14

Glossary 17

Index 18

Many people can't tell which of these animals is a wolf and which one is a coyote.

Can you tell?

They both have sharp teeth.
They both have fur.

They both live in the **wild**.
But which one is a wolf? And
which one is a coyote?

Size

Wolves are bigger than coyotes. They are about three feet tall. They weigh about eighty pounds.

Coyotes are smaller. They are about two feet tall. They weigh about thirty pounds.

Heads

A wolf's head is bigger than a coyote's. Its nose looks like a rectangle.

A coyote has a smaller head. Its nose looks pointy like a triangle.

Feet

A wolf has bigger feet than a coyote has.

11

Food

A wolf eats big animals like deer or moose.

A coyote eats small animals like rabbits or mice.

Hunting

A wolf always hunts in a group or **pack**.

A coyote hunts alone or with one other coyote.

Do you see any wolves?
Do you see any coyotes?
How can you tell?

Glossary

pack: a group of wolves that live together

wild: things that people do not help to grow

Index

coyotes, 2–5, 7, 9, 11, 13, 15–16
deer, 12
hunting, 14–15
mice, 13
moose, 12
rabbits, 13
wolves, 2–5, 6, 8, 10, 12, 14, 16